# Brown is the bear
# in his rocking chair.

# White are sheep
# you count in your sleep.

# Here comes the purple grape gang.

# And their chum, lavender plum!

# This pond is blue.

# The sky is too.

# This fish is light green— isn't he keen?

# Red is for apples big and round.

# And crows are black.

# Trains on a track.

**I'd like to think
most pigs are pink.**

# Color the horse gray, of course.

# Frogs prefer to be seen wearing green.

**Yellow for sunshine
is always fine.**

**Light orange is the color of the moon in June.**

# Tan is the color for Nan and her fan.

# An orange cat is best like that.

# Brown is best for a spotted hound.

# Red is the color of a fox in a box.

# Gold, a good color for fish I'm told!

# How do you do!
# A blue kangaroo!

**Black is the cat
in a witch's hat.**

# Introducing Mr. Lean Green string bean!

# Gray is the color of Miss Mouse in her house.

# Yellow is the color of this little fellow.

# The boy is two so color him blue.

# These fish are keen. You can color them green.

# The road to town is long and brown. Color the car and the road.

# His name is Fred so color him red.

**Color the rainbow using Red, orange, yellow, green, blue, indigo, violet in order. The first letter of each color should tell you which color to use.**

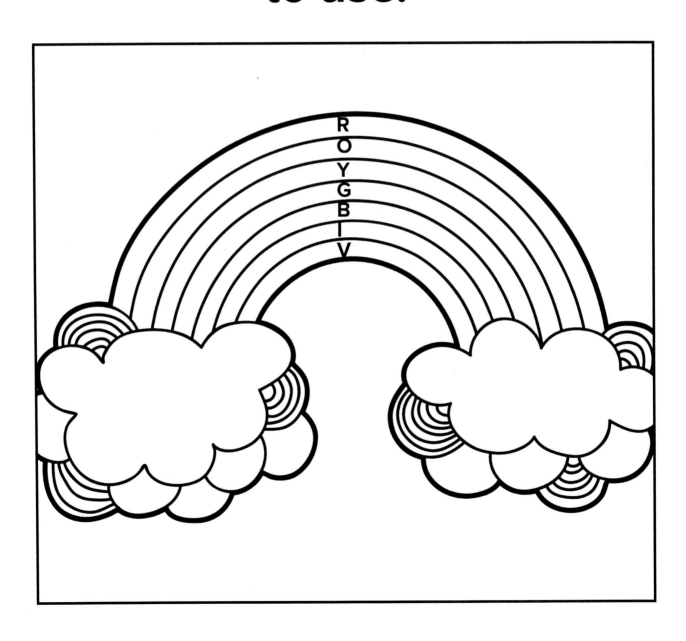

# Color this picture using as many different colors as you can.

# Color the cat with a fiddle and the cow jumping over the moon.